WALKING INTO GOD

WALKING INTO GOD

E. D. BLODGETT

Contributions by
Susan McCaslin, Sheila Martineau, Yukiko Onley

FAIRLEIGH DICKINSON UNIVERSITY PRESS
Vancouver • Madison • Teaneck • Wroxton

Published by Fairleigh Dickinson University Press
Copublished by The Rowman & Littlefield Publishing Group, Inc.
4501 Forbes Boulevard, Suite 200, Lanham, Maryland 20706
www.rowman.com

86-90 Paul Street, London EC2A 4NE, United Kingdom

*Fairleigh Dickinson University Press gratefully acknowledges the support
received for scholarly publishing from the Friends of FDU Press.*

British Library Cataloguing in Publication Information Available

Library of Congress Cataloging-in-Publication Data

Names: Blodgett, E. D., author.
Title: Walking into God / E. D. Blodgett.
Description: Vancouver ; Madison : Fairleigh Dickinson University Press, 2024.
 | Summary: "E. D. Blodgett's final volume of poems, Walking Into God, is
 the culmination of the poet's lifelong devotion to a poetry and poetics of
 the sacred. The poems in this volume present as a single long poem that
 explores the processes of walking, moving, changing, and evolving within a
 unified field"—Provided by publisher.
Identifiers: LCCN 2023057190 | ISBN 9781683933410 (paperback)
Subjects: LCGFT: Poetry.
Classification: LCC PR9199.3.B54 W35 2024 | DDC 811/.54—dc23/
 eng/20231228
LC record available at https://lccn.loc.gov/2023057

for Irena

Now that death has finally entered me,
I must bid you farewell, my love …

Alles vollzieht stumm, einsam, weltabgewandt.
—Theodor Fontane (1819–1898)

Everything takes place silently, lonely, world-averted.

CONTENTS

Part Two:
The Silences

May 2018 – Oct 2018

FOREWORD

Where Does the Voice Come From?

by Susan McCaslin PhD

What interests me in poetry is the interplay of language, the page, and silence. Heaven falls out of words because possibility is in the page, another kind of heaven; I wonder if that's the only heaven we are given to know in life. —E.D Blodgett.[1]

E.D. Blodgett's final volume of poems, *Walking Into God,* is the culmination of the poet's lifelong devotion to a poetry and poetics of the sacred.[2] His mastery of craft, including cadence and sustained musicality, is unsurpassed in Canadian literature. In the poet's words, "What interests me is the interplay of language, the page, and silence ... As [Rainier Maria] Rilke says, all we can do is listen until the listening takes the shape of words full of layered soundings."[3] Though this volume is divided into two parts (or sequences), these compressed poems present as a single long poem that explores the processes of walking, moving, changing, and evolving within a unified field.

'Part One: The Bagatelles' was written between February 2017 and May 2018, and 'Part Two: The Silences' from May to October 2018. Ted died in November of 2018. The Bagatelle poems were written after he was diagnosed with cancer and was undergoing treatment but had retained hope of remission. Though the term *bagatelle* suggests a light, playful game, Ted foregrounded its musical definition as "an unpretentious instrumental composition."[4] Part One introduces God as a boy and raises the question of how to move meaningfully through time from youth to maturity, spring to winter, vitality to decline. The journey leads into an ever more direct confrontation with loss and absence. Yet this descent awakens the sense of interconnection with the beauty of the world and the love of planet earth.

Part Two was composed after all medical treatments failed and Ted moved into hospice care. Here the poetic landscape darkens and deepens. Together, the two sequences sustain a vital dialectic where presence and absence, sound and silence, life and death, are part of an organic whole in which everything is mysteriously interrelated.

During his last year, Ted emailed many of these poems to a small group of literary friends he dubbed 'the cosmos kids.' I was privileged to be among the first readers of both sequences. He would often speak of how the poems seemed to flow through him as if from a supraconscious height beyond his everyday self. It was as if he were engaging with an otherness that was at the same time his core or innermost being. Because the world speaks through him, and he through the world, he can be called a poet of the Muse. The poems kept arriving, sometimes two or three a day, as gifts he crafted as they emerged, bringing to the process his knowledge of multiple languages and expertise in comparative literature, as well as his love of music and the arts. He could often be heard asking, "Where do the poems come from?" Or, as expressed in the final poem:

> what is this God
> that I am always
> speaking about so boldly
>
> and more where
> does the voice come from
> that I claim to hear
>
> it is the silence
> all around me
> coming out of my flesh ...[5]

Walking Into God holds recurrent images and themes in constant interplay. The figure of a fluid, multi-layered God predominates in both sequences and provides the central connection between Parts One and Two. The speaker is walking into God and God into the speaker in a continuous flow. Recurrent images pulse through both sections: sun, moon, stars, clouds; birds, trees, flowers, grass; earth, air, fire, water. Metaphors such as the *gate* as a place of passage and *silence* as a form of divine presence return in new configurations. These figures of speech circle and spiral, linking the two movements in what might best be called a cosmic dance.

As I read the Bagatelle poems in the context of their relation to the Silence poems, it became apparent that Ted was working more as a lyrical poet and musician than as a philosopher or theologian. His use of minimalist three-line stanzas—along with alliteration, assonance, consonance, distanced rhyme, oxymorons, cadence, and sonic word play—creates a fluid musical structure by which he introduces a theme and repeats it in varying contexts. Symphonic motifs appear, disappear, circle, shift, and reappear in a transformative process.

Though Ted capitalizes 'God' and uses the masculine pronoun, the poems are neither patriarchal nor exclusively western; nor are they monotheistic or systematically theological. The presences of Rumi and Buddha—along with allusions to Taoism, Islam, Sufism, and Zen—reveal the poet's interspiritual perspective. In Sufism, which Ted explored through his translations of the Sufi mystic Rumi, each of us in our deepest core is in a sense God, the Beloved, the Friend.[6] As in the mystical poem 'The Conference of the Birds' by Sufi poet Farid ud-Din Attar, in Ted's poems God is as much a bird as an anthropomorphized figure. As he expresses it, "if the garden / has a mind / it is a hummingbird."[7] He draws on perennial wisdom traditions to unify the immanent and the transcendent, the temporal and the eternal, the earthy and the paradisal. His approach rejects a dualism between creator and creature, body and soul, matter and spirit, revealing 'that which is' as ever new songs springing out of silence. The poems embrace the 'God-word' while also challenging and expanding narrow theological notions of God. They reveal that this divine figure is not omniscient, omnipotent, or solely masculine but, rather, what First Nations people call Great Spirit. God, within the poet, experiences awe and loss and even disorientation. By tracking his personal transition into death, the poet explores his vulnerability as co-extensive with the vulnerability of God.

With Ted's inclusion of the feminine in God—as mother, sister, beloved, holy ghost—he denotes that God transcends gender divisions.[8] Yet, God is not a being outside the world but a universal presence in the earth and in all things. God is the hidden wholeness of the poet, residing both within and beyond social constructions. God's cosmic-temporal walking is what one of Ted's favourite poets, Rainier Maria Rilke, calls gazing "out into the open."[9]

As readers enter the world of these poems they might wonder, 'who is the *you* being addressed?' Sometimes it could be God and sometimes the reader. When I asked Ted this question, he responded, "For me the *you* is primarily my wife Irena. All of my poems are written for her." And so the figure of the poet's personal beloved is another appearance of the divine feminine in *Walking Into God*. The personal *you* and the ontological *thou* are one.

Part Two of *Walking Into God* walks us into the mystery of death, facing 'the dark night of the soul' of which John of the Cross speaks. It is a path requiring letting go, *kenosis* in Greek; the release of the constricted self, the passage through fear and confusion to embrace mystery. The poems seldom reflect despair and certainly not cynicism. They affirm through suggestive imagery and metaphor that goodness, beauty, and love are not abstractions, but incarnate here and now. At the same time, they suggest the presence of an ineffable reality beyond the grasp of linear frameworks.

Even under duress, the poet refuses to shape his subtle and fleeting intuitions into a systematic theology or a mystical metaphysics. The poet and the God of whom he speaks are intertwined. They are part of ultimate being. They remain vulnerable, suffer and ponder loss, and question the meaningfulness of their place in the world. Yet, as a whole, the poems suggest that to die into unknowing is to open to a new kind of freedom, a release, even joy, to a "nirvana that empties itself / growing more / and more joyful."[10]

The term *mystical* for Ted is tied to mystery, unknowing, but not a vague obscurantism or mystification. He works within what have been called the *apophatic* streams of western and eastern contemplative traditions. The western paths that spoke most to him are those of Dionysius the Areopagite (5th–6th c.), the anonymous author of *The Cloud of Unknowing* (English,14th c.), and his favourite minimalist, the Zen-like European poet monk, Angelus Silesius, author of *The Cherubic Wanderer* (German 17th c). Ted evoked Silesius to honour his wife Irena in the epigraph to *Apostrophes VIII: Nothing Is But You and I:*

> Nothing is but you and I; and if we two were not,
> Then is God no more God and heaven would be naught.[11]

The dream-like poems of *Walking Into God* enact ways of experiencing a unified reality within all creatures and things that is often unspeakable, not fully containable in our nets of words; yet awe-inspiring in the interplay of sound and silence. The poems you are about to enter sing and point—gesturing beyond themselves, inviting entrance into a cosmological whole.

Susan McCaslin PhD
Fort Langley BC

Notes

[1] E.D. Blodgett, Email message to Susan McCaslin, 29 August 2013.

[2] E.D. Blodgett, "Sublations: Silence in Poetic and Sacred Discourse," in *Silence, the Word and the Sacred,* eds. E.D. Blodgett and Harold Coward (Waterloo ON: Wilfred Laurier University Press, 1989), 207–20.

[3] Blodgett, Email.

[4] "Bagatelle," in *Oxford English Dictionary* (Oxford University Press, 2001).

[5] E.D. Blodgett, "what is this God," in *Walking Into God* (in press), 136.

[6] E.D. Blodgett and Manijeh Mannani, *Speak Only of the Moon: A New Translation of Rumi* (Santa Monica CA: Afshar Publishing, 2014).

[7] Blodgett, "if the garden," in *Walking Into God,* 110.

[8] Blodgett, "when she leaves," 128.

[9] Rainier Maria Rilke, "Duino Elegy Eight," in *The Selected Poetry of Rainer Maria Rilke,* ed. Stephen Mitchell (NY: Harper & Row, 1982), 193.

[10] Blodgett, "more than anything," 102.

[11] E.D. Blodgett, *Apostrophes VIII: Nothing Is But You and I* (Edmonton AB: The University of Alberta Press, 2019).

PREFACE

For Irena

Now that death has finally entered me, I must bid you farewell,
my love, a word I never wished to speak to you, never fitting
how we spoke, and so I must go forward slowly, searching bit
by bit what path in this dark wood to take, but in a forest old
and well travelled. I think of the poets who could not see
the barest difference between love and death, too short-lived
to know that love, the truest wife of life, rises like a slow
moon, to rest above the heart disarming death, its light breathless

and serene. That is the light that speaks to us and then enters us
when first mine and then your heart will break, mine collapsing
but yours barely opening where mine is taken into yours
leaving a scarcely visible line, the seal where you and I become
the we we will remain until time ends, our heads always at rest
one leaning upon the other, our eyes gazing into who
we are, and when you speak, your breath and mine will rise and fall
as our breath, and what you say only saying us, where

the wood, its darkness given up, spreads out in flowers beneath the moon
carrying your words into its light. Walking is easy here, gentle
as the phasing moon, drawing in and then letting its breath
go, teaching the heart in its hours moving through open air,
flowers alone beneath its feet. All the silence it creates
is ours, all the music rising and falling from its pace is ours,
your heart slowly rocking mine beneath the lullaby the moon
makes, all the light only ours, our our ours.

Ted
Easter Eve
31 Mar 2018

Note: Ted wrote this deeply poignant poem without Irena's knowledge, and he instructed
his editor to include it as the Epilogue in his next book only if he was deceased, which
is why and where she first saw it *(Nothing Is But You and I*. Edmonton: The University of
Alberta Press, 2019). The poem was read aloud at the Celebration of Ted's Life and Work at
VanDusen Botanical Garden on Sunday 31 March 2019, exactly one year after he wrote it.

walking slowly

into spring

like walking into God

walking slowly into spring

walking slowly
into spring
like walking into God

nothing that you see
belongs to itself
or anything

the soul you thought
that lay in the river
or any other myth

but we belong
to that breath
floating through the stars

the rain shrouding us
each of us
where light sleeps

under the stars

tracks in the snow

under the stars
a boy flying a kite
dreaming of grace

a dream that says
I am a bird
a bird of paradise

dreaming of saints
of many colours
floating over him

tracks in the snow
of rabbits or
the brief traces of birds

memory lies there
as it in us
barely unfolds

a word we knew
someone's face
someone walking away

silence is our home
lying down
rustling in darkness

how often clouds pause

how often clouds
pause against the sky
nearly rain

someone walks
in silhouette
along a far horizon

a slow shade
uncertain of the port
it has reached

or has the sky
wandered off
a passing homeless rain

an absent-minded rain

an absent-minded rain
that passes by
with barely a nod

hardly reaching grass
before departing
becoming air

not rain but merely
a sigh heard
after it is gone

spoken for stones
for still ponds
and for forgotten things

depart now in peace
all the gates
open wide

to see the sea   **wherever music sings**

to see the sea   wherever music sings
coming and going   silence awaits
its sighing never ceasing   as if the moon

or the sun   were sleeping inside the sun
rising and setting   or the snow
and then rising again   lurked in air

and each of us   each a dance
quietly breathing   the sea upon the shore
without giving it thought   your eyes alive

all of us   where God walks
possessed of God   dreaming what he sees
the breathing without end   tuning silence

harder to speak of yellow   **on the bridge in Avignon**

harder to speak   on the bridge
of yellow leaves   in Avignon
falling in the fall   people dance a round

that light that grows   underneath
lighter in the sun   all the fish
a thinner sky   dart around themselves

transparent grass   in the sky
nothing not exposed   through the night
where stars emerge   the stars turn on north

enigmas of   Sufis spin
heaven given up   dancing nowhere with
there angels   the cosmos alone

and there the dreams
you thought were dreams
unfurl their wings and fly

the open of all things
falling as leaves
and stars fall

how naked the winter trees   **old willows**

how naked the winter trees
their leaves gone
bark exposed

the beauty that they make
traced against
the palest sky

loneliness
falls in the light
no one to take it in

the road home
is where absence is
and open air

and birds that might
have nested there
retreating into dusk

old willows where
the stream pools
and swans turn

Moses may
have floated here
before meeting God

and seen the universe
a passing cloud
open for him

no more gravity than
the rising moon
willow leaves

a universe
of turning children
wheeling round the sun

the small bells
that ring inside your heart
are barely heard

as if afterthoughts
of night fell
over the sea

or birds that fly
into the absence of
afternoons

the laughter of
children not yet born
might ring so

the pure subjunctive of
holiness
and still time

the pure subjunctive of

holiness

and still time

the light that falls   **discarded parts of the world**

the light that falls
on Dürer's hands
comes from beyond the sun

a light falling
without afternoons
or the *there* of stars

the seeking of their prayer
the only prayer
their praying seeks

the only light
that they are given to know
the first morning

the quick light
of gravity
rising without shade

discarded parts of the world
when Matisse was done
lay on the ground

emptiness
where poetry stands up
began to dance

how many coloured birds
hung on branches
upside down

and floating to heaven
the saints beheld
God shaping paper

who will see the swan

who will see the swan
that singing must
depart unseen

a music that remains
silence singing
when recalled

music as
a white ghost passing
or seeming to pass

a song of swans
and rising in the distance
plumes of smoke

that when seen
seems to compose a swan
inaudible

heavy with forgetting

nothing else as quiet

heavy with forgetting
the autumn trees
give up their leaves

all thought
taken away by light
returning nothing

mere specks
against the sky
birds going out

something calls
the voice falling
from bright emptiness

loneliness of the sun
to carry it
upon our hands

nothing else
as quiet as
the trees of childhood

standing where
all the gods stood
before they fled

all there is to know
of stateliness
they possess

every spring
the setting suns
at peace upon their branches

they live in dreams
holding the sky
the day given back

the chestnut trees

elsewhere is not a place

the chestnut trees
leaping up and up
toward God

the stairs their prayers
climb upon
the songs of small birds

what steps are made for us
to make our way
heavenward

for us the smaller tears
the dew leaves
before the sun

elsewhere is not
a place upon a map
but it is there

it has its own trees
its spring and fall
and lost sun

under the trees
your childhood
is always passing through

it smiles as if
knowing who you are
then turns away

the place you occupy

because the place
you occupy
is between heart and hand

you find yourself
in that paradise
where birds fly into words

if you think
there is a way out
you are deceived

all outside
cannot be reached
between hand and heart

the world turns
paradise stands up
and birds speak

the tower bell rings

all flowers

the tower bell rings
tolling the hour
marking silence

all the towers
keep time
until the end of time

between the first bell
and the last
we find our way

walking in the sun
along the shadowed roads
our feet in silence

all flowers
bear in their blood
the long stroke of time

the bells that ring the hours
merely counting
dead at heart

but flowers are
the one measure
opening under the sun

their turning the turn
that time takes
unfolding toward the light

the breath that God breathes
somewhere alone
breathing flowers

all across the light

all across
the light of afternoon
starlings sang

so many notes
for one bird
it was the tree that sang

and all the chestnut trees
that stood on the hill
it was the white

form of flowers singing
the white fire
the *the* of spring

it was the white

form of flowers singing

the white fire

the *the* of spring

beside the sea

she stood beside
the sea singing
ave maris stella

it does not rise
like other stars
but burns night and day

burning as
snow might burn
dancing against the light

no one hears
the sea singing
of such burning light

but homeless birds
who flying sing
across eternal seas

as on a spindle
music running out
and running back

the sorrows of trees

the sorrows of trees
that rise in the mind
beneath a fine rain

and inescapable
the sound of it
like bare breathing

a music of
autumn through poplars
or just the breath

of one remembering
a death perhaps
or what absence

alive at night
slowly becoming
without the least sign

growing old

no other way

growing old
is not for you
but immortality

unfurls on your breath
the breath of flowers
and bright water

bees befriend you
and passing birds
find their way through you

do not fear
the coming of the night
heavy with stars

whose light rolls over you
its deeper breath
sustaining yours

if there were
no other way
to take the sun in

let this be it
to fall until
there is no way to tell

where the gathering web
begins or where
it falls apart

or if the weave
of sunlight is
all there is to be

all the poems   **the one flower**

where to place
all the poems
that are or will be made

consigned to paper
or left viva voce
or simply shelved

where to place
the air your smile has
at the end of day

the light that spreads
across your face
as if the sun were setting

nothing to
hold in place
but how the light stays

breath that on your face
briefly moves
and moves on

the one flower
that I saw
sprang up behind my eyes

sun and rain
played over it
and bees held its life

not for me
to know the fragrance
that flowed into the air

merely how it stood
facing east
toward the sea

the breath of prophets
where children play
their laughter of falling stars

a music that gives birth

Buddha never weeps

a music that
gives birth to silence
flows slowly from your face

a silence that
like a tree
stands upon a sea

through its branches
birds at home
their chanteys the sea's breath

how many ships
pass it by
the sea alone in their eyes

a tree where music
takes its shape
the singing not to be heard

the Buddha never weeps
merely laughter
filling his soul

no sunset
brings a tear
or children lost at sea

he sits inside
the dream he has
of Buddha dreaming the Buddha

only the waking world
held in sorrow
the drift of time

all the herons stand

along the shore

as still as saints

all the herons stand

all the herons stand
along the shore
as still as saints

is this the look
of paradise
a sea without wind

trees where allegories
fail to fall
through empty air

but all the birds
bend at dusk
murmuring their prayers

so enchantment falls
as snow falls
in white sighs

every day

every day
dawn approaches early
in your hair

across lakes
waves follow
a music beyond hearing

a music of
slow waking
where stars disappear

the opening
of the flowers
follow it into light

prayers cannot
capture it
music of light and awe

sweet little juncos

snow between rows

sweet little juncos
flitting through
the end of summer

your hands at rest
upon a basket
carrying the light

where do you come from
quick little juncos
and where do you go

how silent your hands
asleep in the sun
flowers spilling light

snow between
rows of poplar trees
without tracks

the sun the one
presence on the snow
and still air

any bird
flying through
entranced in white silence

a song etched
against a blue sky
seeking spring

as if you bore

as if you bore
the saviour of the world
you entered the room

but no one saw
what you held
and so you went away

music holds the world
and no one hears
the singing moon

the smaller bells of stars
that hold the birds
awake and mute

rain departing
laying bare
the beauty of the world

the smaller bells of stars

that hold the birds

awake and mute

one might exhale

one might exhale
a whole world
in one embracing breath

only a sleeping god
might dare dreams
that utter stars

celestialities
that no one sees
and silent flowers

a sleeping god
whose waking takes
all without regret away

the burning stars
the modest rose
in their eternities

rain through the willow

rain through the willow leaves
trickling down
into a lake

how pliant
are their tears
bending with the wind

everyone has stood
beside this shore
bent by the wind

barely the last   **no more than grass**

barely the last   to be no more than grass
of all frailties   pale and sad
butterflies   where lovers lie

passing by   whatever passes
leaving the still air   over it
opened and closed   it sings amen in green

bearing the fate   in you the earth breathes
of their mortality   the sun in
unperturbed   unfailing and slow

following   St Francis in his death
the endless o   became of grass
of planets and the stars   a naked leaf

                                    and those who pray
                                    their lips are strewn with grass
                                    its longing enough

through a door

so stately stately fall

like stepping through a door
you did not know
had been a door

and stars when first seen
alter the dark
ex nihilo

stars must be
more than stars
and nearly little gods

bells toll
and music leaps from air
grace unbound

so stately stately fall
the autumn leaves
that coast to ground

what beauty lies
in death's pale arms
what quiet breath

how far the sun
standing motionless
above the lakes

what distance falls
from birds that disappear
in plangent cries

what distance falls

from birds that disappear

in plangent cries

the edge of hearing

against the edge of hearing
geese passing
through the dark

it is the way of air
to dream so
of winter's silence

of birds who leave
a wake of just
remembered music passing

all the old towers   **inside the falling snow**

all the old towers
stand on the hills
their bells gone out

above a river
mist hides the sun
dampens birds

the winter leaves
forgetting how it was
they last drew breath

snow will cover all
the air without
the space of colour

stories seem
to fall apart
unspoken from the end

inside the falling snow
an apple tree
barely in bloom

impossible to know
whether snow
or petals fall

or if they fall at all
the air still
with petalled snow

or if the soul of snow
were apple trees
in first flower

sunday afternoons

sunday afternoons
all at rest
to the last leaf

every tree
enfolding providence
a lotus asleep

a cool stream

a cool stream
flowing past
the small stand of trees

flowing with the pace
of music played
with sleeping hands

playing with
the turns it takes
beneath the dreaming trees

music of late light
rippling through
shadows of stars

to gaze on old walls

to gaze on old walls
in the slow light
of afternoons

and brick arcades
where birds escape
into sepia shade

a memory
of summer flowers
falls through the air

someone calls
the sound of it
of flowers and the light

the leaf that falls　　　　　　**it seems asleep**

the leaf that falls　　　　　　it seems asleep
unfolds the air　　　　　　this bluff of old oaks
that rests upon your hands　　　　shaping the sky

rooms where you sat　　　　do they feel the sun
even when empty　　　　its warm breath
know where your shadow lies　　drifting over their leaves

late afternoons　　　　and should they dream
changing light　　　　only birds
where you breathe　　　　enter the dreams of trees

nothing now　　　　sometimes at dusk
known to be lost　　　　a sigh passes between them
stars holding the sky　　　　and heaven speaks

　　　　　　or perhaps
　　　　　　a rush of wings
　　　　　　that whisper unknown tongues

dogs at night   **a cat in the sun**

dogs at night   a cat in the sun
live for stars   licking her paws
the passing of the moon   taking in the world

all of them   her wide eyes
invisible   miss nothing
calling through the night   a universe encompassed

how to live   leaves fall for her
so far from stars   the least flower
and dawns of dying moons   seeks her glance

                                 planets astray in the dark
                                 return again
                                 inside her eyes

                                 perhaps in her stretch
                                 a cosmos came
                                 complete and undisturbed

as if I saw

as if I saw
the hidden side of the moon
at last at last

your face rising
in the dusk
pure chiaroscuro

you but you
brought in from where you stand
beside the moon

or stars coming out
beneath rain
their myths intact

the sea deep in thought   **clouds as if**

the sea deep in thought
the wind itself
a mere whim

but who is it that keeps
the sea and wind
all in mind

all lost from sight
as if drawn
into a shell

the moon and all the tides
poised there
where God has gone

clouds as if
suspended high above
Pissarro's sky

if pigeons passed there
they would stop
waiting for time

a time that glides
beneath their wings
simply holding them

waves before they break
pause without
reaching an end

so eternity
enters the world
on bent wings

Rumi you have asked   **the rain that falls**

Rumi you
have asked that I
should just be God

the rain that falls
in my country
falls through the mind

to meet him where
wine is drunk
to sleep upon perfume

daffodils
that lift under rain
still light

you want the moon
to be my heart
the stars to be my couch

who is there
who does not walk here
with certain steps

to be my childhood
the same trees
the same skies

almost with grace
smaller birds
stroll from seed to seed

how to know
where to place my hands
and what to do

where are we all walking
inside the rain
inside us

where are we all walking

inside the rain

inside us

as many stars

as many stars
as are above Greece
above us

stars possessed
of all mythologies
possessing us

choose but one
that one shall be ours
and we its

a trinity
that places us
wherever the moon moves

stars possessed

of all mythologies

possessing us

stepping into air   **the voice is yours**

stepping into air   the voice is yours
where to place   I hear at night
innocent feet   gliding through our sleep

inside the air   such accompaniments
emptiness   follow alone
no place to place a hand   those who are blessed

we consider stars   no Orfeo
there is the place   carries music so
no path in sight   lifting air

and what paths we have known   and each note
cradling flowers   becoming breath
lined with trees   the being of us inhaled

but we their leaves
thinking we
were left to invisible winds

how to be
such simplicity
the stars so far

the three trees

the three trees
that Rembrandt etched
are always before our eyes

bands of rain
fall away
obliquely on the left

a bearded man
enters from the side
unsure where he is

after so many years
he must have found
the way to us

where now he is ours
and we his
wisdom ravelling rain

wandering manuscripts

wandering manuscripts
of Timbuktu
flutter in the sun

no more than birds
that lose their way
between night and day

flying up
and flying down
the sun losing its path

weightless weight
of the word waits here
reading itself

fireflies of Korans
lighting the heart
of all the heavens

the singing stars
fragments of surahs
finding themselves

traced on the sky   **the calling of trees**

traced on the sky
trees where I was born
leave their wake

and traces of birds
that have slept there
living on

upon the clouds
where no leaf falls
everything rests

winter trees
where the wind sleeps
beside time

the calling of trees
is but to take a shape
that gives thanks

and to embrace the sun
its holiness
taking breath

for you and me
another tree
bears up in our light

innocence
could be all this is
in our eyes

or perhaps God
who cannot speak
but falls mute like leaves

a mere glance

a mere glance
to see ourselves
upon a windowpane

unable to look away
eyes inside
each other's eyes

to gaze upon
trees rising there
filling our eyes

like trees reflecting on
a summer stream
giving it pause

a mirrored mind of trees
our mind
the stream in our eyes

unable to look away

eyes inside

each other's eyes

you touched my eyes

you touched my eyes
and instantly
I saw inside the rain

only to see
there is no rain to see
but merely embraced

as one might be
one with rain
its shadows falling away

beside your bed

beside your bed at night
an angel stands
invisible

her breath falls
over your face
lifting off its pallor

before dawn
fleeing light
she slips inside your heart

and when you wake
impossible to tell
who is angel

your hands lift up

your hands lift up
into the breathing air
and great light

standing on the sill
where eternity
and time meet

the moon surprised
turns between your palms
and huge seas

you and the moon
embraced and held
distant skies come home

pilgrims are what we are

pilgrims are what we are
walking on
beneath the skies

what can the trees say
they wave their leaves
as we pass by

no shrine draws us on
merely our feet
walking on

the shrine we seek
is our shrine
that moves in us alone

the holiness
that it sheds
our pilgrimage

walking toward
each other now
and when stars appear

the stillness of spring

the stillness of spring
cannot be seen
only slowly inhaled

as perfume under the sun
luxuriates
flowing away

stillness then
horizons just beyond
any grasp

there I have seen you gaze
as if you saw
perfume fall

the passage of it then
entering you
where stillness flowers

who can see wisdom   **as one might say**

who can see   as one might say
wisdom walking   you are mine
backward through the world   your voice the breath of dusk

so shy   and see below your feet
always withdrawing   an autumn stream
to hide beyond the stars   pool in the shade

or where silence   too dim to see
when music rests   a face gazing back
slips away inside   from still waters

how might I   but still the stream
be wisdom that you seek   gazes back
in that silence   echoing you

where birds murmur   where you become
inside a hedge   both yours
one appealing to another   water and air embraced

the light of moons
suns that answer
resonance of stars

the apple trees

someplace

the apple trees
around Valais
arise as if dreamt

their petals hang
like hesitant snow
unable to fall

or is it the dream
that hesitates
longing for more sun

a sun that will
rise white
a higher orchard of light

how familiar it seems
to walk there
your hand in mine

the sun lifting us
the strange snow
the dream open

someplace
a memory
of place without place

birds dart there
uncertain till
nestled where they fit

but saints
among their holy trees
walk in legends

and birds stand
unmoving there
each alert to their place

when dawn comes
you dress in light
rising inside the sun

the leaves that fall

the leaves that fall
from these trees
fall without care

into the long
cloud of all unknowns
and sweet grass

when we were children
we believed that we had fallen
from the stars

falling as leaves
from unbelievable trees
in paradise

where one day we
floating slowly back
would be new leaves

above clouds
returning to trees
the only shade ours

the shade that falls
and rises up with us
among stars

deer grazing

deer grazing
that gaze at us
where the wood meets the grass

late afternoon light
glides over them
like thin rain

in such light
shade is all that is seen
the substance of it

the eye of God unseen
but grazing inside
the gazing deer

its light falling over us
passing through
into the deeper light

the eye of God unseen

but grazing inside

the gazing deer

PART TWO: THE SILENCES

May 2018 – Oct 2018

walking into God

is if one walked

into a tree

walking into God

walking into God
is if one walked
into a tree

even if we
walked so
how can we see him

walking through air
lambent and
invisible air

here reason fails
and to walk into God
is to walk through stars

a slow walk
as into music
where no one touches the ground

not knowing
where God is
but moving how music falls

through us
as if we were
falling with the rain

where does it come from

where does it come from
the light that shines
through your face

if not the sun
or ambient air
and dappling shades of trees

none of these
has its shape
a bare breath of light

this is light that gives
birth to doves
rising in dusk

no shade
touching them
nor any other light

where does it come from

the light that shines

through your face

a small gate

a small gate
stands open
in the middle of a field

no one knows
how it arrived
or just exactly when

but finding a way in
the human heart
the dawn eternal

we stepped through
and sat at home
the morning light familiar

the field that took us in
the one that we
alone had grown

and we the flowers
that sprang from us
exhaled from the nearest stars

relentless the waves

relentless the waves
that fall from the sea
pooling on beaches

why is happiness
so complete
in this place

and so what it is
a long stretch of sand
without trees

as if it were
the only way of things
under the sun

where angels must have walked
a word still ringing
round their heads

from far light
unfailing falling
over the sea

lifting the earth
the where of stars
and shadows of the moon

somewhere near

somewhere near
the centre of
the being that we are

a pond lies
beside it willow trees
their leaves dabbling

perhaps fish
perhaps merely shadows
barely moving

side by side
we see but one
figure floating there

a figure we
have never seen
but how familiar it is

without it none
of what we see
and all that stands beside it

all would be
the unseen air
our absence palpable

mountain above a cloud

mountain above a cloud
nothing beneath
but naked air

nothing that
held it there
as if it stood on smoke

a careful eye
will see climbers
walking on the side

but how did they reach
this mountainside
the snow fallen from stars

elysium suns
where they have always walked
or played or slept

the suns they stroll through
that never rise
and never set

contentment falls

contentment falls
like snow falls
beneath windless skies

warmth envelopes you
a young sun
upon your flesh

deep from childhood
your full heart
stretches out

no cat enjoying
the heat more
spilling over from you

this might be all
the grace there is
the grace of suns and cats

simplicities
of such warmth falling
through your flesh

we embraced

we embraced
holding the moon
as closely as we could

but neither sun nor moon
could make us one
merely in light

what spirit but
eternal childhood
could do so

calling to us saying
I am you
you are me

singing in
the heart of all birds
and through us

why do hummingbirds   **perched above a stream**

why do hummingbirds   perched above a stream
ride branches   starlings sing
in high winds   with bright voices

perhaps to follow the dream the flowing water
eagles dream   trickling beneath
on huge wings   murmurs lightly

or higher still   no child
to reach clouds   plays so
of unknown exotic flowers   unpredictably

or finally the stars   bird and stream
where other hummingbirds   dancing like
dart in the wind   lovers in the sun

weightless and free   and the sun
no other desire   dancing with them
than to drink of holy flowers lighting up the air

                             a universe almost
                             falling askew
                             in scattered light

our hands groped

the bird of memory

our hands groped
reaching through heavy leaves
into darkness

sometimes the bird
of memory gazes back
to see what's before

the light of the moon deceives
the edges of things
disappearing

to see me
as a boy
and you before you were born

and the clouds
which shroud the world
in shadow unfathomable

deep in the bird's mind
waiting awaited
and then it sang

how to find
the way to you
all guides gone

a song that came
from somewhere near its end
providence exhaling

or is our guide
our invisible heart
lying where

to come upon us
in its fabled coda
entering the bird's mind

the moon always moves
its tracks
all we have

a memory unfolding
backward and forward
a bird forever migrating

to lead our hands
into the dark
of cloud and shade and moon

through the world
phoenix moon
its mind at home in us

we woke to find

we woke to find
we had become a book
that people carried around

and all of it
was one thing
each word one

even ideas
that might have seemed at odds
were made whole

like a carpet
where all the threads
were woven together

so if it said God
it would be you
it would be me

we woke to find

we had become a book …

so if it said God

it would be you

it would be me

room for prayer

there must be room for prayer
deep and moving slowly
down the river

all of it
holding the words
that poets carefully speak

to reach the ground
where grass comes forth
the roots of all the trees

where each of us
desires to enter
to dress inside such words

what longing is this
to be the prayer
that draws you and me

and we become the words
that others murmur
their deep longings

entering the silence
the amen of each
praying soul

some offer prayer

some offer prayer
their palms up
facing toward the sky

others lie
prostrate on the ground
embracing grass

for us prayer
is how we are
standing in the sun

the silence of it
falling on us
as rain or light will

we do not pray
but we are held
close together by it

and all we say
is yes as fountains do
as they descend

prayer

is how we are

standing in the sun

phoebes cannot move

phoebes cannot
move through grass
in any other way

the walk must be
a ritual
possessing all of us

and you and I
have learned it
straying into ritual

the walking around
of all life
the revelation unhidden

a prayer that we
have stepped into
unknown and unknown to us

the words of it
not words at all
but what breathes through

the breath of all
breathing things
ours and not ours

rising and falling

rising and falling
through the garden
swallows leap with joy

so bold their flying
is how they pray
given to light and air

what they pray for
is mere being
flying enough

their eyes brimming
with golden light
wings open with joy

here is wholeness
the air unfinished
wherever they are not

the air itself
learning prayer
from birds leaping through

tell me where   **somehow we**

tell me where   somehow we
eternity stands   had slipped inside
in what corner of time   a flower in full bloom

where children walk   our legs were held
searching for   within the stalk
whatever is forgotten   seized within the flower

scanning the new   we could see
eternities of stars   meadows of grass
and their surprises   the setting of the sun

laughing at   otherwise
all the heavens   unable to move
changing before their eyes   and given wholly to fate

where God stands   so to be
unknown to God   merely beauty's breath
among the new stars   hanging from stars

how do we know **all we are**

how do we know
that we walked side by side
before you were born

only small
angelic shapes
given eternity

yet we had stepped
on the tilt of time
where time moves on a curve

time allowing
love to thrive
while not seeming to be

and we beneath
holy trees
stood in happy rain

time without
gravity
flying like a small bird

all we are
is that breath
that enters us like light

coming through us
the first summer sun
and both of us

barely born
divinities
leap quickly into it

enough to be
suspended
over the deep valleys

is this how birds
come to be
simply reaching out

the beauty of their
coming into being
the beauty of light

that in its first
arrival at
the very beginning of time

when both of us
and all birds
fell out beside us in air

our bright explosions
the making of light
and our divinity

when you arrive

how did we learn to lie

when you arrive
I always say
now you are here again

here is all here
the birds sweeter
the leaves deeper

and when you are gone
like a stream at summer's end
the heart wilts

what is this but
the inhalation of the world
lifting trees

and its release
birds settling to nest
as the sun sets

knowing it
or not knowing
our breathing follows

and our breathing
lifting and falling
with the passage of the birds

your leaving
with their sleeping
their seeking of the dark

growing smaller
with the early moon
all here gone

how did we learn
to lie for years
on the great open sea

how did we learn
the pleasures of
sleeping on the shore

and finally
the great peace
that comes with giving thanks

all of this
must have brought us to
what butterflies are

to some large
metamorphosis
where all is God

those who have

those who have
been near God
never hear farewell

everything they know
rises up
like a leaf of grass

fledglings are
and early leaves
God's only offspring

and we who are near
have no age
but sit at God's feet

learning words
unknown to us
and full of new greetings

everything they know

rises up

like a leaf of grass

the Tao we are given

the Tao we are given
is open in our hands
like a small book

and written in it
are no words
merely spatial breath

that flows through us
turning us
to see the smallest things

things that
do not lead
but keep the world in balance

and so with ease
we place our steps
even where the stars are

for us the dark
has no fear
but carries its own light

and something hints
at where our feet
might move

without thought
our eyes closed
our bodies given in

garden snails

garden snails
their shells gleaming
in the rising of the sun

the spirals that cover them
calling to
galaxies beyond sight

but both held
in the constant turning
of eternal folds

where God in all
his convolutions hides
cosmic and Sufi

near the smallest birds
that hop past
always surprised

divinity
that moves with
a pace that stops time

we emerge
at galactic speed
gleaming round and round

in late summer

in late summer
the trees
their leaves asleep

God himself
seems to sleep
and all that lives and breathes

as at a great breath
were let out
and nothing inhaled

such enchantment
can only fall
through the whole of space

and we gaze
at each other
as creatures almost blind

what greater divinity
rises then
from the sleeping earth

a wakefulness
that holds the smallest
things in longer light

the gate opens

the gate opens
the being of God
with all of us beside it

a small fence
leading from its unearth
but nothing closed in

childhood
seems to rise
like a special breath

and on the breath
doves that rest
on air and light and all

that floats up
from being and
the gentle open gates

who would dare
speak of stepping
through the gate that opens

soundlessly
and all who walk there
walk into the unknown

but sense they walk
into who they are
and what they have not been

and cannot help
but sing what they know
and never have sung before

the green passage
of time brought
into a light

never seen before
but grasping us
with a love unknown before

never seen before

but grasping us

with a love unknown before

a centre without

a centre without
the least centre
but only a long dispersion

going nowhere
wherever nowhere goes
just apart

like stars without
the shape of constellations
merely lights

if divinity
has a bottom
this might be it

but even such
an end cannot
be wholly counted

is this to be last
or rather truly forward
everywhere

you walk through

when Tolstoy grew old

you walk through
the garden like
a nun in contemplation

nothing can disturb
the still flow
of your thinking

a tree might grow
inside it and
it would not have noticed

you are their soil
when their thinking takes shape
grown with your roots

these holy trees
of your mind
filling with green shade

when Tolstoy grew old
spring around him
flourished as never before

the young shoots of poplars
and puffs of clouds
delicate and young

I think he was drawn
through the seasons
especially the first warmth

the prayer that
skims off the tip of the day
the prayer of age

that celebrates
apple blossoms
falling from the stars

how radiant   **everything we see**

how radiant   everything we see in God
the tulips that leap toward   we have put there
the silent sun   without asking

the slightest change   and all that we believe
of light becoming   but God is where
a new line of colour   emptiness dwells

divine dialogue   the silence of it
across the great distance   a silence unbelievable
of empty space   and great stillness

whose reverence   no story will
springs up   explain why
with joy on every side   it is how being is

a radiance   no saint in sight
on every face   no space for any desire
becoming tulips and sun   but breathing perhaps

how do we know

where owls sit

how do we know
if we have fallen
to the bottom or

just apart
given nothing as
a certain guide

when as a boy
I fell down
dazed into time

like a young bird
a wing damaged
swept from side to side

o to call
and hear that what is called
are all the cries

eternity might make
coming into birth
for the first time

its wings untried
crawling though
all of space unknown

where owls sit
somewhere inside
wherever God is

and where is God
if not inside
the God where God sits

their fall unhampered
into all the divinities
where God resides

and all the enigmas
refuse to be unravelled
merely calling

from the deepest music
the night speaking
the start of stars

in many corners

in many corners
of our garden
puffs of wind fluttering

that are the white
flags of butterflies
flitting about

small flurries
of frailty
appearing in spring

first tentative
steps of the cosmos
abandoned to the air

how small amid
the entrance of
the stars and moon

what is the pace

the first bird

what is the pace
that God walks
and where does he walk to

how does distance
spread before him
and how does the elysium mean

where he moves
do these questions
have any meaning at all

what colour does
the moon have
for him or any star

and if he dared
to touch any of them
would they last

the first bird
that may have seen God
cock his head

the way birds see
what might he
have seen first

especially looking
for small seeds
and seeing only stars

is this where thought
first arose
staring at what was never

seen before
and did God
return the bird's gaze

and gazing begin
the holiness of the world
their awe shared

the light that came

a world with new breath

our souls the place

how long God

how long God
must have slept
after the world began

missing Adam
and Eve and the sons
perhaps the flood

and did she dream
what happened instead
all the families unfolding

and so many
animals
with all their longing music

and what if she
when we were born
came to life again

the light that came
a world with new breath
our souls the place

where stars began
the sun flooding our bodies
born of the sea

walking into the world
not knowing its
divinity

new for us
never still for God
just waking

perhaps God is   **if God dies**

perhaps God is no more   if God dies
than a storm   does divinity
of white snow   die with him

like the Tao   and how are we
that has gone off   to have a glimpse
in all possible directions   of what we might have been

how to tell   standing between
them one from another   two fields of absence
God content   without a sun

to follow the Tao   without the gift
in its farthest point   of choosing one
where it fades away   where the wind stripped the leaves

into itself   and night falls
as if into   without the grace
the darkest part of the sun   of moonlight going forth

                                    if God dies
                                    what prayer comes
                                    to remember what has gone

and how to wake

and how to wake
into something never
seen before

a light unknown
and to lie down
inside the darkest dark

overwhelmed by fear
where a mere star
opens the cosmos

to dream again
and where to cry for help
before prayer

came forth
from a silence that
would bring the star to God

the loneliness

the loneliness
of divinity
cannot go deeper than this

of God peering at
the world for
the first time

how quickly courage quails
trying to grasp
empty air

what is it for
is all that can be asked
and where is God

to stand in what
must be beyond
any measure

divinity without
any shapely
outside

chaos waiting
to be born
the first passage of light

and so God woke

and so God
woke again
to feel the world moved

it could not be described
other than
to say it seemed

to move around itself
God moving
around with it

powerless
but to follow it
and the round air

putting chaos to rest
hidden somewhere
where God goes round

God had not yet

God had not yet learned
how to stand
only the cosmos

with its dim light
unfolded without
the slightest movements fumbling

and as its dance began
shadows first
of unforeseen

figures arose
only their shadows
giving shape to the world

no other purpose known
arising in silence
where all that moved

was air dancing
and shadows in the dark
of what they were shadows of

the only words

the only words
the cosmos knows
are of deepest gratitude

no matter how much
God in the sinking dark
loses his way

but a way out
has no more sense
than knowing where north might be

and what would north
mean to God
or wind or placing the sun

what is God to do
where light rises
simply by itself

and when the moon
goes to its place
and lanes of lindens appear

where God in a dream
learns to walk
along the lines of trees

beginning to wonder
what dream
is the dream that leads to cosmos

everything that is

everything that is
is the cosmos
waiting to be

and when the birds
entered into their new song
God drew

his own first breath
and the cosmos shook
but the first shock

was God's own
his breath drawing all
near to him

suddenly in
mountains leaning toward
his open mouth

the sun almost
falling from its orbit
and all the stars

God at last
finding his first words
and the first rain

beginning to fall
across his face
joy his first word

Saint Francis spoke

when Saint Francis spoke
all the birds
in the garden sat up

then a bird
that speaks in your heart
and spoke in mine

and while deeply at home in yours
began to sing
as never before

giving the long hymns
from Saint Francis
that make us whole

where stars take their rise
the moon full
on the horizon

and we are no matter
how we look
only alive to praise

dreaming of animals

how much he loved

dreaming of animals
that had not yet
seen life

God's hand
groped against yours
and placed it carefully

on my cheek
where he held it
until my eager skin

no longer felt
like skin but something
putting holiness on

that came over me
as the first day
the world knew

the light it carried
filling me
with the breath of new love

how much he loved
the morning sun
that spread across the hills

but most he loved
the cries of children
running joyfully through light

but how could God
pray for what was his
from before time

and who would pray
for what God loved most
beauty passing

the children disappearing
or perhaps himself
walking out of time

who knows how

who knows how
to lift stillness
and carry it past the sleep

of God into the forest
nothing not even
the air disturbed

whatever at prayer
in complete unknowing
stillness unbreathing

and we who are made
in that image
graver than the soul

and his train of stars
we who strangely
begin to fly

without the image of birds
stillness that sings
the light of light

when you leave

when you leave
I cannot help
but reach to hold your hands

as if they were
the hands of God
still busy with creation

just come
from the depths of the earth
warm and soft

freshly mingling
with new dirt
your hands and his

becoming one
and what they might say
more intimate

than words
brought each night to me
roots enfolded

a small pond

a small pond
where the wind
in slow sarabandes

riffles the still
surface of
water holding the moon

everyone gazed
and then forgot
what they were praying for

perhaps prayer
was not needed
merely standing there

and everyone looked
at each other
and saw that they were the prayers

the silence around them
coming from
the breath of prayer that

had created them
nothing to see
but stillness of praying air

complete silence

complete silence
and another heard
with murmurs from everywhere

as of poplars in
the summer air
but speaking in tongues unknown

o it is snow
before winter
begins to lie beside us

and from the silence
not the chatter of children
nor what was once

echoes of
old wells
and murmurs of multiple tongues

but simply us
our eyes the same
slow inhaling of silence

small poplars
of the spirit
that we have been asked to be

God has no reason

God has no reason to be
invisible
to hide in his

divinity
except in his beauty
he may be so dazzling

that all that moves
may suddenly stop and stare
unable to bear

the beauty passing by
but wonder now
whether this

was just a show
God being able
to take on any shape

and we unable
ever to know
what it is we see

more than anything

more than anything else
prayers fly
bird-like past us

and so the air speaks
filled with desire
everywhere

but prayer that is
utterly selfless
rising from the deepest ground

of absolute and breathless
lakes of silence
where being lies alone

such prayer prays
only to itself
asking for nothing

nirvana that empties itself
growing more
and more joyful

how much depends   **seeing God go by**

how much depends   seeing God go by
upon so much   still a boy
that passes us unnoticed   curious

but when seen   and pausing for
quietly loved   the smallest creatures
beginning with the air   that slip around his feet

that settles on the sea   not knowing how closely
clouds that are   they belong to him
nearly sky   and he to them

children unseen   their movements still
calling from afar   rituals like his
and beyond all   miniature dances

a gesture somewhere   perhaps this is how
holy in its heft   we all learn how to move
lifting the moon   into the sky

and you lying in the lift   becoming the birds
not knowing where   that carry in our souls
you have arrived   the new cosmos

becoming the next
of other moons
caressing the casual tides

I write these poems

I write these poems
a letter every day
and hand them to you

they rest first
in God's hands
and then in yours and his

poems open
evangelically
holding the poem

together with words
that seek the sweetest
melodies to be found

duets that summon up
divinity's
singing light

I write these poems

a letter every day

and hand them to you

if anyone can be blind   idly lying beside

if anyone   idly lying beside
can be blind   a small stream
certainly   God dips

God can be   her small hands
in front of all   into the cool water
the uncertainty of the world   a smile forming

unable to tell   in her eyes
what light might be   how much of this
or where the sky is   simply flows through her

the cosmos perhaps   how much is her
only apparent   the bright stones
as music interweaving   the shimmer of the surface

its lines alone   trees bend over her
drawing the planets   to touch first
into their mysterious circuits   and then bless

where just   this holiness
the finest voices   gladly at rest
bare of ornament   praying for the world

lay out   nothing sings
the invisible universe   like she sings
that he might touch   her mouth full of stars

only to hear   rising one by one
how it sings   in the jubilant voice
through the unwavering dark   where the sun rests

no one has embraced

no one has embraced
God or stroked
his dreaming face

the loneliness
must be
as infinite as he

as he passes by
trees turn
slightly away

even the air
holds its breath
and birds pause in flight

no one knows
where he sleeps at night
behind the moon or star

nothing we want to know
possible
to bring to mind

I wonder what

I wonder what
the moon smells like
after God

has spent the night
sitting there
contemplating all

that passes in
the dark beside him
and the sweet smell of flowers

rises everywhere
no one can speak
but only cry out

thank God
for all that flowers
become in holy fragrance

God is thought

God is thought
to have a sister
tall and soft-eyed

during the day they tend
the humblest flowers
especially the clover

at night they speak
a language no one knows
of places unheard of

where is God
where is his sister
and where are we at night-fall

without them in the dark
how cannot we speak
without prayer

God is thought

to have a sister

tall and soft- eyed

to be blinded

to be blinded by
morning light
unable to know

what might be
in front of him
but stepping forward with

temerity
losing sight of where
the planets were

he knelt and prayed
as he knelt
he felt the wings of birds

unknown to him
moving past
in such a way

that did not feel
like what they were
as fear came over him

and kneeling and holding his head
how close God came
to losing his way

the cosmos slipping
from his grasp
heaven getting lost

if the garden

if the garden
has a mind
it is a hummingbird

but one so swift
she's rarely seen
the mind invisible

of all the garden it contains
and there God
must find his way

groping through the dark
only a flash
of a passing bird

but one surge of breath
from her swift passing
and all the shadows

begin to rise up
filling darkness
with other birds

each entering the mind
of God to be
the cosmos he now

must bear
in fear and awe
of what the bird might be

how could we know   **simply bees**

how could we know
the shape God
preferred to take

was that of a hummingbird
nothing so quick
that needed not to fly

merely to think
to follow its thought
and being there where

thought and bird
becoming new being
and taking wing

joy to be
upon the verge of being
anything

or simply bees
that fly in God's shade
how are we

to know how they
feel when the sun
begins to reach out

stroking their soft bristles
following the flowers
where God sits

the fragrance that spills
over them
is more than they can bear

uncertain if
this is God
or what they want him to be

a place to sleep
between flowers and the deep
smell of God

no one speaks of angels

no one speaks of angels
as they used to do
perhaps they have

nothing to do
what news of holy births
summons them

and where were they
when light first shone
across surprising hills

so they were needed
but only now and then
they came on a whim

perhaps that's all
we need them for
to arrive when both are thought of

yet what we thought
was merely sacred
rose above the sun

lifting us
where holiness
without angels prevails

when God goes home

when God goes home
where does he go alone
nowhere to go

does he possess
a house where he lies down
fully at ease

perhaps a stand
of chestnut trees
that he has always loved

or maybe just himself
a solitary house where he
stands alone

but his feet move
softly over grass
where the wind pauses

where birds have nibbled
through the day
and small rains have dropped

home a gathering of light
caresses where
graceful touches

hold the daze
of divinity
in their pensive hands

God seems now

God seems now
to be no more than old
memories

of childhood
and other idylls
brought back to mind

or memories
of what the future might
perhaps become

but God stood up
like an apple orchard
yet where is he

a God of falling apples
in the fall
or of the snow

that cannot be escaped
and at last the air
that must be breathed

and when breathed
bringing eternity
into sight

the moment

the moment God smiles
the light that fills
the universe

changes how
it illuminates
wherever it falls

even shadows
fill the air as if
they smiled too

a smile not to see
but rather a
fleeting caress

falling across
whatever lives
beneath the darkest rivers

of all blessings
bearing the simple
happiness of God

one day God awoke

one day God
awoke to find
he had become a leaf

not a feeling
but a kind
of long emptiness

and being helpless
hanging in the wind
at that point

of just being
blown away
at slightest gust of air

and lost somewhere
among the stars
with no homeward light

that brightens being
returning it from the edge
of lost things

one day God

awoke to find

he had become a leaf

such deep pleasures   **when the sun had set**

life holds   when the sun
such deep pleasures   had set without
no matter how brief they are   being noticed at all

perhaps it's because   he heard a voice
they are so well remembered   rarely heard
despite the longest   a woman who sings in the dark

absence of many years   a voice like
and our hands quietly   his sister's full
touch again   chromatic variations

as God lays   singing in a whisper
his warmly over   beneath the quick shivering
ours in deep blessing   of acacia leaves

a blessing that has   hymns that had
no way of saying   not been composed before
any farewell   but simply fallen

but is carried   sweetly from her lips
wherever God   and God thought how
might choose to move   the softness filled

eternity the way   the universe
he breathes upon hands   with new music
bound together   bringing him to his knees

the turning leaves

the turning leaves
of the fall the first time
o did God dream

this coming to pass
the fire of colours that leap
through the trees

as if spring
had not yet returned
how does this happen

this turning of time
to make it now uncertain
to know the when

of where one walks
back and forth in time
and when God wakes

he wants to see
autumn in its first
brilliant colour

all turning
causing him to dance
the universe

inside him
the first Sufi
letting time go

but when God smiles   **God was listening**

but when God smiles
what smiles
if not the trees

that line his path
the earth where he walks
the grass where his feet dance

God does not
own his smile
it is bestowed on everything

in the end
what does God own
he is God

because he possesses nothing
free of what
might be his

God was listening to
Mozart in late
afternoon

and as he took in
all the music
he knelt in reverence

and standing beside
him a pair of angels
held their breath in awe

what can be said
of how the air
expands in holiness

birds hear it
beginning to sing it
with familiarity

until the whole cosmos
is filled with Mozart
and happiness

taller than the trees

when God saw

taller than the trees
God stood
gazing at the pale

sky that seemed
to fade into
its infinity

almost something he
could touch
and next to him

his sister in the late
light beside
birds that listened

to God's voice
beginning to sing what he
sang until

the air was full
of the new song
of spring still to come

when God saw
from the light he saw
that he was not the light

but staring into
the light he saw
at last where he was standing

what does it mean
not to be the all
and what is he able to know

what to create
and what to make it with
not recalling

how he made
the zebras and if
he failed or if the stripes

were wrong o the first
prayers in the cosmos
God's cries for help

the desire to be

the desire to be
a bird was sometimes
irresistible

not a special
flock but just one
that hid in the hedgerows

yet the music they made
was unforgettable
and when they float

gently beyond
the clouds and high
behind the distant stars

it troubled God
that he was not already
born a bird

a flash of beauty
with nothing to do
but give beauty away

beauty enough
to be holiness
merely a song

and when God said

and when God said
let there be light
who was he speaking to

as if he had asked
let there be a moon
who was it for

since God has no needs
even to ask
for the dark

how can the desire
to see the universe
be enough to create it

enough to give
permission to the sea
to pass by

God took Buddha

God took
Buddha by the hand
and walking together

they stepped into
a nearby forest
and in the darkness were

unable to
tell who was who
God or Buddha

both picked up
a small stone
that was their shared nirvana

both knew
on the spot
now they were merely breath

and all the air
around them blew
slowly through them both

emptier
than all space
but breathing everywhere

unable to

tell who was who

God or Buddha

when God was still   **God was walking**

when God was still   God was walking down
in his early years   a dusty road
in the world   invisible

he spent hours   to all who might
gazing at its beauty   be looking at him
and the quiet air   leaving nothing but

the birds that passed   a track of dust
back and forth   like any boy
beneath the new trees   who has lost his way and lost

he was sure   himself and lost
he had not made   what he might look like
all these things   if someone saw him

especially beauty   'how to be God'
above the pool   was how an old prayer
where reason lies in peace   used to begin

and so he wondered   especially if God
where he was   seemed no more
and how he just appeared   than a swirl of dust to those

perhaps just waking up   who need to know
the world merely   where he is
standing around him   and what his grandeur is like

what sacred breath
exhaled all this
life entering the world

the first fall

before God grew old

the first fall
is so beautiful
it can only be God

to walk into it
is so overwhelming
that the first time

stays inside you
forever wherever
God chooses to be

unattainable
but always present
inside the snow

ours but not ours
its beauty everywhere
the air filled

with the small flakes
of an eternal fall
of purity

before God
grew old
passing the afternoon

while sitting beside a pond
remembering his youth
sprawled in the sun

he lost the sense
of what it meant to be
the sun enough

to let him feel
the passing of time
time feeling the same

young or old
the light air
and age a mere breath

gracefully exhaled
autumn colours crossing him
changing

how many minds

how many minds
how many eyes
how many ears does he have

how to tell
autumn in the north
from all other autumns

we are without compass
wherever we look
we look nowhere

how do we know now
whether God sees where we wander
through shapeless seasons

how can we know
how to pray
knowing nowhere to travel

we are without compass

wherever we look

we look nowhere

beneath the pale

beneath the pale
cloudless sky
the last breath of summer

exhaled slowly
through the trees
perhaps this is God's

sister caressing
all living things
the air bearing

my eyes toward yours
where the late roses
flower as if

that was how
they beneath
the blue sky breathe

when she leaves   **nothing so peaceful**

when she leaves
where does she go at night
the holy ghost

no one remembers
seeing her
whether night or day

perhaps a part
of her dwells
in all of us somewhere

each of us
joined to the deepest
divinity on the verge

of all things
dancing on the moon
tripping on stars

the ghost of God
the ghost of holiness
the ghost of ghosts

nothing so peaceful
as twilight over
a waveless sea at dusk

is this the holy ghost
or God waking
in the stillness

you would think
that only the air
is drawing its own breath

everything else
moving back and forth
in holy twilight

nothing certain
what is God
and what is holy ghost

God in the end   **of all the moments**

God in the end
is not what a wish
might be but rather a placing

geese departing
the exact smell of your hair
a child's smile

doing what must be done
to open the way
of shaping the world

until all is placed
for beginnings to
come into being

your first birth
a crying out
across the deepening void

of all the moments
without the reverence of God
it is the moment when

the stars appear at night
across the sky
but in silence

where is God's laughter
where is the joy
that should greet

their bright coming
the moment everyone
feels their overcoming

of darkness and God's
not once taking
them deeply into the rapture

of night illuminated
and the heart of laughter
filling the cosmos with joy

God's first compass

God's first
compass was
without any north

and so we
began lost
and we will never know

where we are
when he gazes
at us across the cosmos

what is the prayer
for lost souls
when even the trees do not know

where they are
and God walks
in circles unable to

find himself
beneath the moon
and where o where the evening

appearing somewhere
unknown and we
fade into dusk

someone might ask

someone might ask
what is the figure
called God who always appears

if not the everywhere
that cannot be touched
or otherwise known

the hibernation of bears
the sleep of sloths
forgotten clouds

how do we pray
to this unseen figure
everywhere around us

where does its guidance come from
to take us by
the hand to lead us

across deserts
uncharted skies
and seas that are lost

when God came into   **the simplest of things**

when God came into the world   the simplest of things
he must have been   to enter a polar bear cub
as befuddled as we were   to prepare for winter

no one recalls   God's first winter
the loneliness of the day   on your back
the absence of creatures   carrying down the sky

but that was the first day   and if you listened
and awesome silence   closely enough
filled the air   you might say he cooed

no other way   giving the air
to celebrate the day   its softest hues
face in the grass   pale blue fading

no hallelujah   and what is this bear
just gentle reverence   but darkness praying
and soft amens   rising from beauty

it had not rained

it had not rained
for centuries
and this disturbed God

who loved rain
especially fine
rain falling slowly

when nothing gets
really wet
but barely moist like mist

but where to go
in the long drought
where land would disappear

and he felt too
that he must become a smaller
and smaller desert

older poplar trees

at the top of older
poplar trees
God loves to sit

and gaze at sparrows rustling
through winter light
changing from

pale blue
to darker yellow
God never so much

at home remembering
his old age
before it arrives

God was a little boy

when God was a little boy
he had a desire
to be a sparrow

small and swift
happy from branch
to branch in constant glee

what he loved
was chatting to
the other birds that learned

to laugh among
themselves full of all
their youthful vigour

perhaps never to be other
than to lie on his back
dreaming of sparrows

and perhaps he
without purpose
staring into an empty cosmos

the meadow had fallen

the meadow had fallen
into such deep warmth
you found it hard

to move except
for the open gate
appealing to you to enter

and when God stood
holding open the gate
his eye was only

on the far horizon
where he could
contain the sun

so that it could
not stray far from you
or from his eye

lying in the double holiness
where God and the great stars
shine from pleasure

what is this God

what is this God
that I am always
speaking about so boldly

and more where
does the voice come from
that I claim to hear

it is the silence
all around me
coming out of my flesh

yes my flesh
where all my secrets
remain nearest to me

secret flesh
holy flesh
flesh waiting in silence

where

does the voice come from

ACKNOWLEDGEMENTS

I am deeply grateful to all the friends who supported my husband's creative spirit in his last days; to the nursing staff at The Irene Thomas Hospice in Delta BC who cared for his physical and emotional well-being, freeing his mind to commune with his muse; and to our family members who gave emotional support when it was most needed.

I also want to sincerely acknowledge the contributions of those who helped shepherd this book through to posthumous publication:

- Dr. Peter Midgley, Ted's friend and Literary Executor (and past Acquisitions Editor, The University of Alberta Press);

- James Felton, founder of Poets Corner, a Vancouver-based poetry reading series, for his determination and unique sense of organization;

- Prof. James Gifford, Director of Fairleigh Dickinson University Press (FDU) – Vancouver campus, and a colleague of Ted's throughout his academic career;

- Zachary Nycum, Associate Editor at Rowman & Littlefield in Lanham MD, a co-publishing partner of FDU;

- Susan McCaslin PhD, poet, writer, educator, and editor, for editing the manuscript and writing the Foreword;

- Sheila Martineau PhD, writer, copyeditor, designer, and social researcher for designing the book's cover and page layouts;

- Yukiko Onley, owner and curator of Visual Space Gallery, who photographed the cover image and Ted's favourite portrait.

My personal thanks and special appreciation are further extended to James Felton, who brought humour and friendship to Ted's final days; to Susan McCaslin, Ted's kindred poetic spirit, who has given me wonderful emotional support during this difficult time; and to Sheila Martineau, one of Ted's spiritual travelers, who did what I could not, extracting the original poems from hundreds of his files and emails.

Irena Blodgett
South Surrey BC Canada

E.D. Ted Blodgett (1935–2018)

Photo: Courtesy of Yukiko Onley © 2005

ABOUT THE AUTHOR

E.D. Blodgett PhD

(1935–2018)

Edward Dickinson (Ted) Blodgett received a PhD in Comparative Literature from Rutgers University. In 1966 he began a long teaching career at the University of Alberta and, as a scholar and literary critic, wrote extensively about, and promoted, Canadian and medieval literature, inspiring generations of students to love literature and poetry.

Ted read widely in many languages and taught in many countries—including Austria, Germany, and France—and in 1986 was named a Fellow of the Royal Society of Canada.

Above all, Ted was a poet who published close to 30 books of poetry, for which he received two Governor General's Awards as well as awards from the Writers' Guild of Alberta and the Canadian Authors Association.

A co-founder of the Writers' Guild of Alberta (1980), Ted also served as Writer in Residence at MacEwan University (2004) and was Edmonton's Poet Laureate (2007–09). In 2011 he was named to the City of Edmonton's Arts and Culture Hall of Fame.

Ted sang with the Richard Eaton Singers, played the renaissance lute, loved birds, and played squash. After he retired as Distinguished University Professor Emeritus, he held the Louis Desrochers Chair in *Études canadiennes,* Campus Saint-Jean. During his retirement on the west coast of British Columbia he continued to sing in choirs, play the lute, travel, read, and write poetry.

Front Cover Image: 'Departure'

VanDusen Botanical Garden, Vancouver BC Canada

Photo: Courtesy of Yukiko Onley © 2005

THE CONTRIBUTORS

Susan McCaslin PhD
English Literature
(UBC 1984)

Poet, Writer,
Educator, Editor

Faculty Emerita
Douglas College
New Westminster BC

Langley BC, Canada

I had the pleasure of first meeting Ted Blodgett at a joint book launch in Alberta in April 2011. Ted became for me not only a towering literary figure, but also a poetry mentor and friend. Receiving drafts of the astonishing poems that flowed through him in his final year and a half was an enormous privilege. Being asked to edit his final manuscript, *Walking Into God,* has been an even greater one.

- www.susanmccaslin.ca

Sheila Martineau PhD
Social & Educational
Studies (UBC 1999)

Writer, Copyeditor,
Graphic Designer,
Social Researcher

Freelance Consultant
& Creative Director
Vancouver BC, Canada

After encountering Ted's *Apostrophes* series in 2003, I was moved to contact him. Fifteen years of his generous mentorship and friendship ensued. What a delight when he'd email a new poem he thought I might like. It has been both pleasure and honour to design the posters for his public readings, the program for the Celebration of his Life and Work, and the cover and page layout of this book.

- www.sheilamartineau.com

Yukiko Onley

Photographer, Gallerist

Owner & Manager
Visual Space Gallery
Vancouver BC, Canada

www.visualspace.ca

I was introduced to Ted in 2004 at a poetry reading he gave in Vancouver. When I had the opportunity to photograph him I asked if he would write a poem about a recent loss in my life. The result was a collection of poems published in *Elegy* (2005) and illustrated with my photographs. After Ted retired to BC he held several readings in my gallery, accompanied by lute music and 'the presence of the divine.'

- www.yukikoonley.com

Memorial Plaque

VanDusen Botanical Garden, Vancouver BC Canada

Photo: Courtesy of Irena Blodgett

a tree where music

takes its shape

—*a music that gives birth,* p. 21

BOOKS OF POETRY BY E.D. BLODGETT

Ex Nihilo. Trans. J.R. Léveillé. At Bay Press, 2021.

Apostrophes VIII: nothing is but you and I. Univ. of Alberta Press, 2019.

Songs for Dead Children. University of Alberta Press, 2018.

Horizons. St. Boniface: Les Editions du Blé, 2016.

As if. University of Alberta Press, 2014.

Apostrophes VII: Sleep, You, a Tree. University of Alberta Press, 2011.

Praha. Czech trans. Athabasca University Press, 2011.

Poems for a Small Park. AU Press, 2008.

Le Poéme invisible/The Invisible Poem. Editions du Noroit, 2008.

A Pirouette and Gone. Buschek Books, 2006.

Particles of eternity. Buschek Books, 2005.

Au Coeur du bois/In the heart of the wood. With Jacques Brault.
Éditions Lucie Lambert, 2005.

Elegy. University of Alberta Press, 2005.

Apostrophes VI: open the grass. University of Alberta Press, 2004.

Apostrophes V: never born except with the other. Buschek Books, 2003.

Ark of Koans. University of Alberta Press, 2003.

Apostrophes IV: speaking you is holiness. Univ. of Alberta Press, 2000.

Apostrophes III: Alone Upon the Earth. Buschek Books, 1999.

Transfiguration. Trans. Jacques Brault. Editions du Noroit, 1998.

Apostrophes II: through you I. University of Alberta Press, 1998.

Apostrophes: Woman at a Piano. Buschek Books, 1996.

Da Capo. NeWest Press, 1990.

Musical Offering. Coach House Press, 1986.

Arché/Elegies. Longspoon Press, 1983.

Beast Gate. NeWest Press, 1980.

Sounding. Tree Frog Press, 1977.

Take Away the Names. Coach House Press, 1975.